To Andrew
with best wishes
David Knight
April 1991

Destiny
An Uncommon Journey

David W. Krueger, M.D.
and
Jane Newfield, M.S.W.

Winston-Derek Publishers, Inc.
Pennywell Drive—P.O. Box 90883
Nashville, TN 37209

Copyright 1991 by David W. Krueger, M.D. and Jane Newfield, M.S.W.

All rights reserved. No part of this book may be reproduced in any form without written permission from the publishers, except by a reviewer who may quote brief passages in a review to be printed in a newspaper or magazine.

First Printing

PUBLISHED BY WINSTON-DEREK PUBLISHERS, INC.
Nashville, Tennessee 37205

Library of Congress Catalog Card No: 90-70570
ISBN: 1-55523-350-3

Printed in the United States of America

*Once, there came into being,
a ship
whose name was Destiny.*

*From the beginning,
she was fresh and full of hope.
There was about her
a sense of forever yet never-before.*

Destiny was lovingly conceived and crafted.
She was finished and polished just so.

To those who looked upon her,
Destiny seemed to shine with pride and promise.

Still,
near her beginnings,
when she was yet being formed,
everything was not as promising as it seemed.

There were, for example, some few details
inside
that were overlooked or missing altogether.

But, she was so well attended
in most important regards,
that no one noticed
the slight spaces
or the places
where she did not join well
with all her other parts.

*Destiny herself knew in each moment,
and to her very core,
that all was not well.*

*But she said nothing
since she was so new, and
it being a time before she had words.*

*And later,
as these things go,
she forgot that she ever knew that she knew.*

*In the same way,
Destiny stopped having her own thoughts
and feelings.*

This is how she survived.

*After all, no one expected a ship
to have thoughts and feelings of her own.*

*Since so much of who she truly was
went unacknowledged,
Destiny secretly vowed to stop needing anything
or anyone.
Or, at the very least,
she pretended not to have needs —

even to herself.

Deep within her, however,
the needs did not die.
They came to reside as a wish inside,
silent and hidden,
that somehow,
someone
would just know
and understand,
without there having to be words.*

But this wish became, increasingly,
more silent,
more secret,
throughout Destiny's formation.

And so it went, that no one,
not even Destiny now,
ever considered that anything
could really go wrong.

What she did know—
the lesson she had learned so well—
was that she was to perform.
She wanted more than anything
to know and to feel
that what she did mattered.

She wanted to be what everyone wanted her to be.

She came to believe that her very existence
depended on performing not only well,
but brilliantly,
as if her performance defined her.

The only way she recognized herself
was when others acknowledged her,
and praised how well she did her job.

For awhile
Destiny sailed smoothly.
She moved without effort through the water.

Her course was determined by various elements.
She responded to the prevailing winds.
When the winds were especially strong,
she was blown about the seas.
She was guided by others
and responded sensitively.

Her own sense of the seas,

born within her,

was one of the fundamental, forgotten things.

It was her mission to look good.
And she became very good at looking good.

Her efforts took so much energy, though,
that she grew increasingly tired.

It was at times like this that she let herself know
that something was missing.
But it wasn't clear what that something was.

She looked longingly
upon other ships which passed.
They sailed without apparent trouble or doubt.
She felt twinges of envy
and pangs of emptiness.

*Since she was accustomed to looking to others
for direction and affirmation,
she searched now in the same manner
for answers to her confusion.*

*Destiny kept trying to find what was missing.
She picked up new passengers
hoping to be happy.
But eventually they all disembarked.*

*She tried to fill her hold with new cargo.
But it did not make her feel full,
only more aware of her own emptiness.
Soon enough, it was unloaded.
It was as if nothing were hers to keep.*

*Happiness seemed elusive,
though somehow attainable.
There were always occasions for hope.*

*She went from port to port,
hoping to find just the right port.
Maybe that would be the answer.*

*But, it was as if she came from nowhere
and had no place that felt like home —
no place she belonged.*

She was now aware of feeling lost.

There were times when she felt
like she was falling apart
and needed to be glued together all over again.

But she sailed past those times,
and into days when the breezes were easy
and the waters welcoming,
sometimes even shimmering in the sunlight.

She could feel happy—
almost.

From painful experience,
she knew that every good feeling
was destined to disappear,
and she would again feel bad.

Just when things were going well,
she was slapped unexpectedly by a wave,
creaking her bow and crumbling her confidence.

This reinforced her belief that,
inevitably,
something would go wrong,
and she would feel helpless and hopeless.
She came to distrust her good feelings.
She was careful not to feel
too good
too much
too long.

Destiny was tired
and she was tired of being tired.
She became angry.

She rejected all she knew,
all the compromises she'd made
just to survive.

This was her rebellion:
she would be as different as it was possible to be
and not care what others thought about her.
She would just please herself,
if only she knew how.

Soon Destiny found herself
more alone
and just as tired as ever,
still longing to belong.

*As she might have predicted
a great storm arose one night.
The rains lashed Destiny's decks,
as if the very heavens
were weeping bitter, stinging tears.
Lightning flashed, thunder rolled.
A howling wind whipped up dark clouds
that raced across the face of the moon
and changed its expression.*

*As frightened as Destiny was,
there was a part of her that was glad:
now with this storm all around her,
she could at least identify
something specifically that was the matter.*

*She remembered her wishes for some tragedy,
to give shape and definition
to her moody discontent.*

*While frightening, the crisis
was a welcome respite
from the nothingness.
The storm was a particular and familiar terror,
thus better than the formless dread.*

*And because others could see it , too,
this somehow made her experience more real.*

*Strong waters,
angry waves
swirled the helpless Destiny about.
It was difficult to tell where she ended
and the sea began.
Each crashing wave threatened to swallow her.*

*Destiny feared for her very survival,
for this storm was different.*

*The strangeness of this storm was such,
that even as the storm about her subsided,
the storm within continued.*

*Although it was a silent, secret storm,
this time Destiny could no longer deny
having sailed so long without her own feelings.*

*She let herself be afraid
all the way to the center of her,
where she knew something vital to be missing.*

*Destiny looked into the now-still waters
to find her image.
She needed her very existence mirrored to her:*

that she was there;

that she was real.

*She also saw reflected
how battered and frightened she was.
And this was real, too.*

*She could now no longer go on alone.
The next storm would be too much for her.*

Destiny wished for magic.
She longed for the time, long ago,
when she believed in magic.

She now knew, painfully and repeatedly,
that magic did not lie
in different ports
or new passengers
or the promise of a rich cargo.

Each had provided the illusion of hope
and seemed to work for a little while,
but never well enough
for long enough.

*This last storm forced Destiny to look
inside herself.
She had not done this for a long, long time . . .
perhaps ever.*

*She realized now that her very structure
must be strengthened
from inside her.*

*Once, it took
forgetting
just to survive.
Now, it would take
remembering.*

Only By Remembering Can You Truly Forget.

*She had to do what humiliated
and frightened her the most:
she had to ask for help.*

*It now took all her strength,
rather than to hold together,
to let go
and admit she needed something—
though not quite sure exactly what it was.*

Destiny went to a different kind of port—
a place known to have helped others like her.

It was hard to put herself in the hands of others.
Her pride,
her very existence
had been in being a performer
who made it through challenging seas
and every storm,
to every port.

It was surprising to others also
when Destiny went for help,
because she had appeared to be so independent.

Destiny didn't have to perform in this harbor,
though she did at first,
simply because it was her way of being.

Unless a performer, she didn't know
who she was.
Unless focusing on others, she felt confused.

Her words were carefully chosen and monitored,
lest she offend and alienate someone important.
She felt constantly afraid
of abandonment by others,
afraid that every bond could be shattered.

The Ultimate Abandonment Is Of Your Self

Her emptiness now seemed intensified, starkly revealed.
She felt more lost than ever.

She feared she would be painfully exposed, as if under a white, penetrating light.

Only By Sharing The Secrets That You Feel Keep You Separate Can You Be Truly Distinct.

*Destiny felt as if she were many pieces
rather than whole.
Pieces of each who made her . . .
long ago.
She felt like a collection of parts
without her own identity.*

*If she were not a composite
of those who made her,
living on in her,
then who was she?
Several components even bore the clear mark
or voice
of someone very important from her past.*

*She knew that she had to fashion
a wholeness and identity—
her own sense of herself.*

To Know

All That You Are

Is To Be Whole,

To Feel Real.

When the work got especially hard,
Destiny recalled her long struggle
with knowing that something was missing
and of being afraid of getting help to find it.
She was afraid that no help existed,
as if what she needed
had neither definition
nor answer.

What was this healing process
that hurt so much?

The magic for which she hoped
was itself an illusion.

She became angry,
for she thought the experts held a secret code
that would unlock her mysteries,
yet were not giving it to her.

For a time,
Destiny attempted to define herself
by rebellion.
She became defiant of all that she knew,
of her traditions,
especially of being good.

Although it took awhile,
she came to see that, ultimately,
her rebellion offered
no greater freedom.

Both Conformity And Opposition Occupy The Same Prison.

With a growing sense of trust,
she allowed her doubts, feelings,
questions, memories
to emerge.

Of all the things she had done actively
to try to feel better
and find what was missing,
she learned that
the most active,
the most nurturing
form of doing something
was to listen to herself.

And she had much to say

and to feel.

It Is What You Don't Know That Makes You Sick.

Destiny had not belonged to herself.

*She reclaimed parts of herself,
forgotten feelings.*

*She saw the neglected
and omitted aspects of herself,
the disregarded pieces.*

*Remembering
Is The Opposite
Of Losing.*

*Grief Is Our Way
Of Communicating Attachment.*

At times,

the pain of her work

surpassed the pain of the storms.

*Bearing The Unbearable Pain
And Seeing The Unseeable Truth*

Are The Same.

*Grief Unspoken
Will Seek Another Language
Of The Body Or Heart.*

The Work Of Mourning Is Remembering.

And then,
as she looked around her,
she recognized ships which she had envied,
now going through their own rebuilding.

Destiny had been watching
one particular ship she admired,
whose work was near completion.
One day she asked the other ship,
"Am I going to be just like you?"
"No," the other ship responded.
"You're going to be just like you,
only more of who you really are."

Destiny continued her work.

*She knew that courage
was not to lack fears
but to proceed despite them.*

*Every movement ahead
was not comfortable in the beginning,
for it was new and unknown.*

*The only way she could know,
certainly and predictably,
was to go backward.*

Though Seemingly Very Close,
The Past
Is A Faraway Land
To Which You Can Never Return.

*Love Which Is Lost Must Be Told,
Not To Be Forgotten,
But To Be Woven Into The Tapestry
Of The Present.*

She filled the empty spaces by allowing
her knowledge,
her experience,
her feelings,
to expand into those places.

She came to know that her emptiness
was created when she abandoned herself
to seek the response and approval of others.

The specialness which Destiny longed for
was not in being different,
or alone,
but in being unique.

It was hard.
It took a long time—
not by the calendar—
but by Destiny's experience.

It seemed to take a whole lifetime.

Finally,
when the end of the work could be envisioned,
a launch date was set.

Strangely, Destiny now feared to enter again
the very waters she had been afraid to leave
only a little while earlier.
She became afraid of the changes
she knew had occurred,
afraid of her new strength.
She feared that if she sailed away,
all her flaws would return.
She was scared of what would happen
in the first storm she encountered.

She was afraid there would always be something
missing.

*Yet, stranger still,
she also feared that there wouldn't
be something missing—
that she would be very different.*

*And she knew that, although the harbor was safe,
ships are not made for harbors.*

She was sad for many things:

for what was,

for what was but should never have been,

for what might have been.

And sad now,
for those whom she had grown
to love and trust,
and must now leave.

*But Destiny knew
she had come to the end of her past.*

And it felt good.

So, rather than looking backward,
Destiny experienced all her present:
all of

here and now.

She even dared to look to the future.
For she knew, deep inside her,
that she was now   whole.

In her search for magic

she had found

her Self.

Destiny had now fulfilled her name.

The End

of

The Beginning